Little Town Band

A Musical Tale by Tom Jahnke

Illustrated by Deb Hart-Chase

To: HARPER + NOLA
CHRISTMAS 2019
LOVE GeGe

A "Little Town" Book

www.LittleTownBooks.com

Tom Jahnke's picture book story, Little Town Band, is delightful. Told in rhyming verse with beautiful illustrations, the story is both entertaining and educational. The band instruments are introduced one at a time, teaching young readers about each instrument, like the "big tuba", the "small silver flute" and the "slick slide trombone slid all over the place". The author uses lots of metaphors, alliteration and imaginative associations to make this story come alive. The reader can almost hear the cacophony of noise produced by this un-practiced town band. There is an important message in this precious story: the old saying that "practice makes perfect" is very appropriate for this little town band.

ISBN 9781543961393

For Jean

Not long ago, but before you were born,

came a noteworthy thought on a bright summer morn.

It was said that a town just wasn't complete,

unless a town band could march down the street.

So in the newspaper 'twas put out a call,

"Looking for Players, Please Come One and All."

Shortly thereafter a group was at hand,

a newly formed troupe called the Little Town Band.

They came from all over, their mission was clear,

to play altogether and make the town cheer.

So before the parade all the players did meet…

They gathered their music and took to the street.

The parade began promptly, the crowd should attest,

the Little Town Band would surely sound best!

The band promenaded and everyone heard,

a clamor that sounded a little absurd…

There was a big tuba
who blew much too loud,

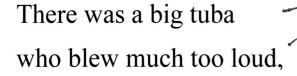

and a small silver flute,
barely heard by the crowd.

The slick slide trombone
slid all over the place,

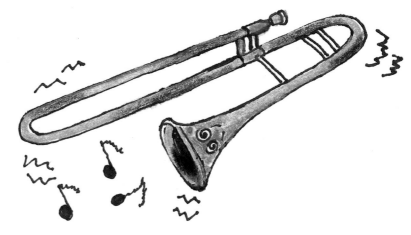

and a clarinet squeaked,
it was quite a disgrace.

A brass trumpet blared,
its tone out of key.

The saxophone wailed
like a cat in a tree.

The bass drum kept thumping
an incorrect beat,

while everyone watching looked down *at their* feet.

The band sounded frightful, the crowd wasn't cheering.

In fact, it was said that someone was jeering.

Everyone wondered what could have gone wrong,

as the Little Town Band kept marching along.

The parade finally ended, the band members knew
that their playing had sounded extremely askew.
"What *could* be the reason?" did ponder the band.
"Perhaps it's our music that no one can stand."

So they got down to business composing new songs,

in hope that their music would sound good and strong.

The town once again had another parade,

but the band sounded *worse* than the first time they played.

"We need to play sharper!" they touted with flair.

"Perhaps uniforms are what we should wear."

So they went out and bought some new hats and new jackets,

in hope that they wouldn't make quite such a racket.

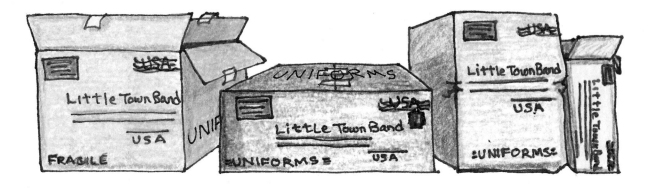

"These surely will help us to play perfectly,"

as they donned their new clothing and smiled happily.

Again the crowd waited for them to begin,

but alas came out nothing but one great big din!

"A new place to play," the musicians did state.

"Perhaps a nice bandstand would make us sound great!"

So they built a large structure with plenty of room,

in hope that their playing would suddenly bloom.

The town brought their blankets and chairs to the lawn
around the new bandstand to sit down upon.
The Little Town Band tried as hard as they could,
but the music, as always, just didn't sound good.

"We play all new music, we built a new stand.

We even wear clothing that makes us look grand.

We can't figure out why we always sound odd

and never the audience will they applaud."

Then out from the crowd came a cute little fellow.

He wore checkered shorts and a shirt that was yellow.

He wasn't much older than seven or eight.

He held a balloon and his smile was first rate.

He walked toward the bandstand and up the few stairs.

He opened his mouth like he hadn't a care.

He asked the conductor a question quite plain,

"Do you ever just practice again and again?"

A silence came over the Little Town Band
as the members looked up from their musical stands.
"Perhaps that is it," they started conversing,
"We haven't spent any old time just rehearsing."

The band was quite happy, no longer dismayed.

The cute little fellow had come to their aid.

He taught them that kudos is something that's earned.

It's important to practice, a lesson well learned.

The band, they did practice and practice each day,

until the next concert was ready to play.

Could all their hard work really make them sound awesome?

They hoped that their playing would suddenly blossom.

Once more, the townspeople did gather around.

They were hoping and praying to hear a nice sound.

The band started playing and to their surprise,

came a wonderful sound bringing tears to their eyes.

The big tuba blew
and it wasn't too loud,

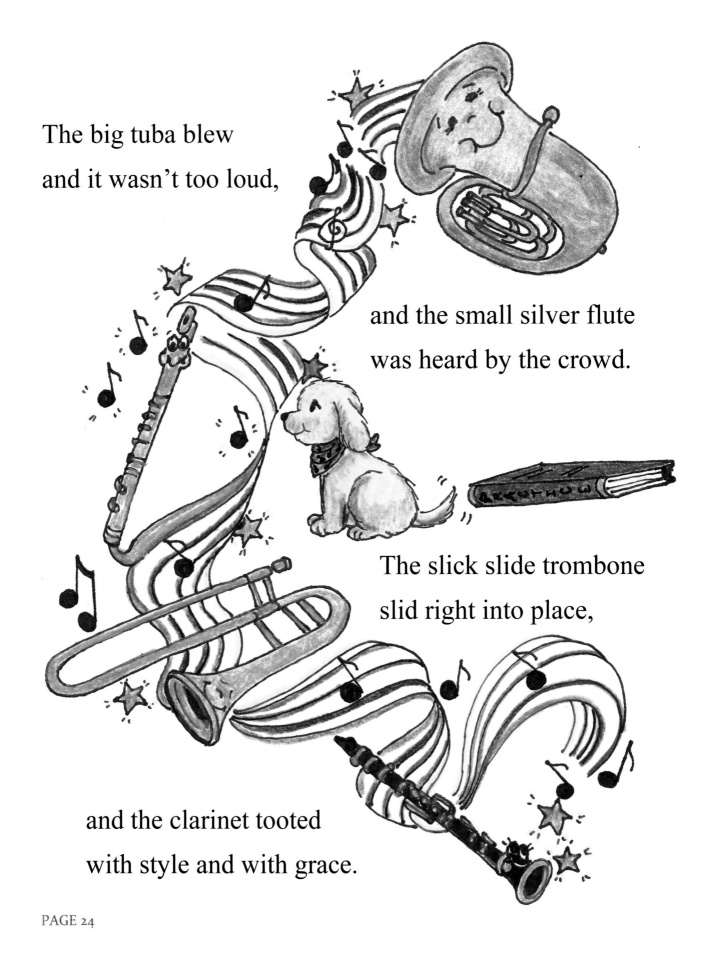

and the small silver flute
was heard by the crowd.

The slick slide trombone
slid right into place,

and the clarinet tooted
with style and with grace.

The trumpet hailed nicely
and in the right key.

The saxophone, well,
just played perfectly.

The bass drum kept
everything right on the beat,

while everyone watching jumped up   to   their   feet!

They whistled and clapped and applauded for more.

In fact, it was said someone shouted "Encore!"

And that is the story, you've heard it firsthand,

why everyone loves the Little Town Band!

And the cute little fellow who started it all?
It's said he's conducting at Symphony Hall.

The End

About the Author

Tom Jahnke is the musical director and conductor of the Chatham Band in Chatham, Massachusetts on Cape Cod which has been playing to thousands of people every summer Friday night since 1932. Starting as a trombone player in 2004, he soon became the band's music librarian and assistant director. He holds an Associate of Science from Massasoit Community College and a Bachelor of Arts in Communication with a concentration in Theater Arts from Bridgewater State College. He is a vocal soloist for the Outer Cape Chorale in Provincetown and the First Congregational Church of Harwich. He also enjoys singing and playing trombone with the Harwich Town Band, the Sandwich Town Band, the Cape Cod Moonlighters Big Band, and the Sound Dunes Swing Ensemble. He has a passion for writing as seen from his column in the Cape Cod Chronicle and is looking forward to publishing more children's books in his "Little Town" series.

About the Illustrator

Deb Hart-Chase retired from the Barnstable School System on Cape Cod, Massachusetts in 2013 after thirty-six years of teaching in the field of Visual Arts. She has an Associates in Fine Art and Fashion Illustration from Mount Ida in Newton, Massachusetts and Bachelor's degrees in Art Education, Fine Art, and Art History from Southeastern Massachusetts University. Deb also has lectured across the country on career education and art integration into all school subjects. She has illustrated close to 20 textbooks along with authoring five books on K-12 art education. She has illustrated numerous greeting card designs for Marion Heath Card Company. Deb currently resides in Centerville, Massachusetts with her husband, Don. They have one son Michael, a recent law school graduate.

Special Thanks

Cynthia McGalliard for making this book possible

Marge Frith

Maestro Peter H. Cobb, Harwich Town Band Conductor

The Harwich Town Band

Maestro Jeremy R. Cadrin, Sandwich Town Band Conductor

The Sandwich Town Band

The Brewster Town Band

Jim Stamboni and the Sound Dunes Swing Ensemble

Bob Katcher and the Cape Cod Moonlighters

Elizabeth Moisan and A Book in the Hand

Don Chase

Chatham Charlie and the Litwins

Sally Davol, Stephen Davol, and Anita Harris

The "World-Famous" Chatham Band

and last, but definitely not least…

My Dad
for attending every performance of every band every week, year after year

In a world of peace and love, **music** would be the universal language.

Henry David Thoreau

Look for additional

"Little Town Books"

Coming soon!

Little Town Christmas

Little Town Choir

Little Town Church

Little Town Park

Little Town Beach